FROM CREATION TO THE GOSPEL

an Advent Devotional

———⪦———

MICHAEL WOOD

Copyright © 2016 by Michael Wood

from Creation to the Gospel
an Advent Devotional
by Michael Wood

Printed in the United States of America.

ISBN 9781498490320

All rights reserved solely by the author. The author guarantees all contents are original and do not infringe upon the legal rights of any other person or work. No part of this book may be reproduced in any form without the permission of the author. The views expressed in this book are not necessarily those of the publisher.

Unless otherwise indicated, Scripture quotations taken from *From Creation to the Gospel - an Advent Devotional*. Copyright © 2016 by Michael H. Wood. All Rights Reserved

Scripture quotations taken from the English Standard Version (ESV). Copyright © 2001 by Crossway, a publishing ministry of Good News Publishers. Used by permission. All rights reserved.

www.xulonpress.com

Presented to

_____

By

_____

On _____

For

_____
_____

**In honor of my Lord and Savior,
Jesus Christ...**

**in His name
and
for His gospel.**

I wish to offer my thanks...

To my wife, Judy, whose support has always come when it was most needed...

To my granddaughter, Alyssa, whose cheerful spirits and bright smiles are always an encouragement...

To my pastor, Keith, who was a willing sounding board and whose comments helped to put on the finishing touches...

But mostly to God who made it possible in the first and last places.

We live in a world that emphasizes instant gratification and commercialism. When these two characteristics are combined, you get a reasonably accurate picture of what the Christmas season has become – fast, cheesy, and shallow.

We need to remember how to relax and slow down so we can appreciate the gifts God has given us
– creation and His Son.

Advent calendars are a wonderful way to slow us down. They give us a way to mark the time leading up to Christmas when we can celebrate the birth of our Lord Jesus Christ.

They also can help us teach our children patience and how to look forward to something with anticipation – to have hope in something in the future. They can help us share our hope of Salvation with those the Lord has given into our keeping to raise.

This Advent devotional is a bit different than others. It begins in the days of Creation when God created man and woman and, over the first six days of December, it covers their creation, the temptation, the Fall, and the curses on the serpent, the woman, the man, and all of creation.

Starting on December 7th and continuing through December 24th, the devotional shares the path from the Fall toward the redemption laid out in Scripture. This path is shown through prophetic promises in the Old Testament and their corresponding fulfillment in the New Testament culminating in the birth of our Lord Jesus Christ on December 25th.

December 26th offers the plan of salvation as a logical next topic after Christ's birth.

The devotional continues through December 31st touching each day on topics crucial to a Christian's spiritual growth and concluding with The Great Commission of Matthew 28:18-20 on January 1st.

May the glorious love of God be made manifest in you and may you share it with others to the fullest.

Dec 1

Made in God's Own Image

²⁶ Then God said, "Let us make man in our image, after our likeness. And let them have dominion over the fish of the sea and over the birds of the heavens and over the livestock and over all the earth and over every creeping thing that creeps on the earth." ²⁷ So God created man in his own image, in the image of God he created him; male and female he created them. ²⁸ And God blessed them. And God said to them, "Be fruitful and multiply and fill the earth and subdue it and have dominion over the fish of the sea and over the birds of the heavens and over every living thing that moves on the earth."

Gen 1:26-28 (ESV)

Some say that God used evolution as the method of creating human beings. This is called The Gap Theory. This Theory suggests that the Creation Narrative spanned millions of years. However, I cannot find in this passage anything to support this view. The Creation Narrative indicates a time span of six days, but that point aside, the aforementioned Theory has evolution at its core. It claims that humans began as protoplasm and increased in complexity, on their own, into primates and finally humans. This point alone removes the Gap Theory altogether. Scripture tells us that God created us "in His own image" and I find nothing anywhere in Scripture that supports the idea that God is bio-goo or an ape. Therefore, we can celebrate the fact that we were not created in the image of, nor did we evolve from, primates. We are God's chosen people. Made different than the rest of creation in that, into us, God breathed His essence and gave us to be His rulers and representatives on the earth.

Dec 2

The Temptation

¹ Now the serpent was more crafty than any other beast of the field that the Lord God had made. He said to the woman, "Did God actually say, 'You shall not eat of any tree in the garden'?" ² And the woman said to the serpent, "We may eat of the fruit of the trees in the garden, ³ but God said, 'You shall not eat of the fruit of the tree that is in the midst of the garden, neither shall you touch it, lest you die.' " ⁴ But the serpent said to the woman, "You will not surely die. ⁵ For God knows that when you eat of it your eyes will be opened, and you will be like God, knowing good and evil."

Gen 3:1-5 (ESV)

The key in this passage is the twist that Satan uses when talking with Eve. He says, "You surely will not die!" In this, he deflects the meaning of God's Word. God was (and is) interested in the spiritual health of mankind and their place in eternity. Satan works to deflect the focus from the eternal and toward the immediate here and now. Sin brings many immediate physical pleasures, but the eternal consequences are separation from God. Sin may bring short term happiness, but being in and abiding in God's Grace (unmerited favor) brings eternal joy.

Dec 3

The Fall

⁶ So when the woman saw that the tree was good for food, and that it was a delight to the eyes, and that the tree was to be desired to make one wise, she took of its fruit and ate, and she also gave some to her husband who was with her, and he ate. ⁷ Then the eyes of both were opened, and they knew that they were naked. And they sewed fig leaves together and made themselves loincloths.

Gen 3:6-7 (ESV)

Many times the beginning of this passage is used to blame the woman for the Fall of mankind and creation. The Fall being when mankind fell from God's Grace and sin entered into creation. However, immediately following Eve's failure, we see that Adam was with her when she ate the fruit. He knew what she was doing was wrong and against God's command. He did not help protect his wife from Satan nor help her remain in God's Grace. He abdicated his responsibility as God's appointed leader, followed her lead, and brought the Fall upon all of creation. Furthermore, do not think that God did not know this would happen. His plan of redemption, that was in place before the foundation of creation, needed something to be redeemed from – and so we had the Fall.

Dec 4

The Curse on the Serpent

¹⁴ The Lord God said to the serpent,

"Because you have done this,
cursed are you above all livestock
and above all beasts of the field;
on your belly you shall go,
and dust you shall eat
all the days of your life.

Gen 3:14 (ESV)

When pronouncing His judgment on Satan, God used the phrase "above all" twice: "above all livestock" and "above all beasts of the field." The key to this curse is found in that creation has the hope and promise of redemption (being reconciled to God by the act of another), but Satan does not. Satan is an eternal being, so when God cursed him for "all the days of your life," it was an eternal curse with no hope of parole.

Dec 5

The Curse on the Woman

¹⁶ To the woman he said,

"I will surely multiply
your pain in childbearing;
in pain you shall bring forth children.
Your desire shall be for your husband,
and he shall rule over you."

Gen 3:16 (ESV)

———∝———

Note in this curse of the woman that God did not remove the blessing of her part in the continuation of the human race. She still has the blessing of feeling a life grow within her, of participating in the raising of the next generation, and knowing that she is still part of God's plan. Yes, He increased the pain she endures in giving birth and yes, He decreed man would be the head of the family, but He did not remove her from His Grace.

Dec 6

The Curse on the Man and Creation

^{17} And to Adam he said,

"Because you have listened to the voice of
your wife and have eaten of the tree of which
I commanded you,
You shall not eat of it,'
cursed is the ground because of you;
in pain you shall eat of it all the days of
your life; ^{18} thorns and thistles it shall
bring forth for you;
and you shall eat the plants of the field.
^{19} By the sweat of your face you
shall eat bread,
till you return to the ground,
for out of it you were taken;
for you are dust,
and to dust you shall return."

Gen 3:17-19 (ESV)

The curse on the man differs from the curses against the woman and against Satan in that the man's curse is not limited to him alone. Because of Adam's actions, and the responsibility bestowed upon him, God cursed all of creation. Prior to the Fall, as Adam tended the garden, the ground freely gave of its bounty, but not so after the Fall. When mankind fell, all of creation fell with him and, until it is fully redeemed, we will experience the consequences of Adam's actions: disease and violence and the pain of losing loved ones to death. We do not live in the Eden of Genesis 1, rather, we live in a Fallen Genesis 3 world, but hope still abides and we can rejoice in that knowledge.

Mankind has Fallen!

No longer worthy to walk with God in the garden in the cool of the day.

But fear not.

God is sovereign.

It's part of His plan.

- Promises -
- Fulfillment -
- Redemption -

Dec 7

The Promise of Victory

¹⁵ I will put enmity
between you and the woman,
and between your offspring and her offspring;
he shall bruise your head,
and you shall bruise his heel."

Gen 3:15 (ESV)

God alone is sovereign (holds absolute and complete power) over all of creation. If there are doubts as to the veracity (truth) of that statement, this verse should set them aside. In the third chapter of the entire bible, God reveals the meat of His plan for mankind and creation. He describes how the story will end. There is no need to skip ahead to see how things turn out. God tells us the end at the beginning – while Satan will inflict pain in and on the world for a time, he will be defeated. This, God knew from the beginning and the only way this could be is that God is sovereign and in control of His creation.

Dec 8

The Coming of Victory

⁴ But when the fullness of time had come, God sent forth his Son, born of woman, born under the law, ⁵ to redeem those who were under the law, so that we might receive adoption as sons.

Gal 4:4-5 (ESV)

Again we see reference to the sovereignty of God – "when the fullness of time had come." This indicates that a time had been set for this event and it happened when that point in time had been reached. Also, God's Son was born of woman meaning that, in addition to being God's Son, He was also from the seed (descended from) of Eve thus fulfilling that part of the promise mentioned in Genesis 3:15. And one more thing, He was born under the law the same as Adam, so that He could fully redeem where Adam had failed.

Dec 9

The Seed of Abraham Promised

¹ Now the Lord said to Abram, "Go from your country and your kindred and your father's house to the land that I will show you. ² And I will make of you a great nation, and I will bless you and make your name great, so that you will be a blessing. ³ I will bless those who bless you, and him who dishonors you I will curse, and in you all the families of the earth shall be blessed."

Gen 12:1-3 (ESV)

Out of all the people in the world God chose Abram (who we know as Abraham) to be the patriarch of the people He would choose as His own. The father of the Jews. The first to bear the covenant (agreement) of the circumcision (a physical mark of obedience). The sovereignty of God is once again in evidence. He said that He would make Abraham into a great nation and, through him, bless all the families of the earth. Sounds like a plan to me!

Dec 10

The Seed of Abraham Revealed

⁷ Know then that it is those of faith who are the sons of Abraham. ⁸ And the Scripture, foreseeing that God would justify the Gentiles by faith, preached the gospel beforehand to Abraham, saying, "In you shall all the nations be blessed." ⁹ So then, those who are of faith are blessed along with Abraham, the man of faith.

Gal 3:7-9 (ESV)

In Genesis 15, God counted Abraham's faith as righteousness:

⁶ And he believed the Lord, and he counted it to him as righteousness.
Gen 15:6 (ESV)

So justification (being declared right with God) through faith was even in evidence in the Old Testament. Christians throughout the ages are the blessing God promised to Abraham. Truly, Abraham's faith in God was a shadow of the redemption that was to come through Jesus Christ.

Dec 11

Heir of David

⁶ For to us a child is born, to us a son is given; and the government shall be upon his shoulder, and his name shall be called Wonderful Counselor, Mighty God, Everlasting Father, Prince of Peace. ⁷ Of the increase of his government and of peace there will be no end, on the throne of David and over his kingdom, to establish it and to uphold it with justice and with righteousness from this time forth and forevermore. The zeal of the Lord of hosts will do this.

Isaiah 9:6-7 (ESV)

Israel's second king, David, was not the richest king nor was he the one with the most glory. However, he was described by Samuel to be the one sought by God as "a man after His own heart." When David expressed an interest in building a house for God, God told him that He did not need a house in which to dwell. He then told David of the legacy that He would give to David's family line: that his house and his kingdom would be established forever. This kingdom, through the Kingship of Jesus Christ, would not be limited to an earthly reign.
It would transcend time and creation and would last forever.

Dec 12

David's Heir

¹ Paul, a servant of Christ Jesus, called to be an apostle, set apart for the gospel of God, ² which he promised beforehand through his prophets in the holy Scriptures, ³ concerning his Son, who was descended from David according to the flesh ⁴ and was declared to be the Son of God in power according to the Spirit of holiness by his resurrection from the dead, Jesus Christ our Lord,

Romans 1:1-4 (ESV)

The genealogy of Jesus in Matthew starts with Abraham and travels through David so the Jews could see that Jesus was the Messiah promised in the Old Testament. But, while Paul makes mention of this required connection to David, he gives further proof of Jesus' Sonship: the Holy Spirit's power and the resurrection from the dead. The genealogy, including Abraham and David, was a requirement set by the Lord through His prophets and thus was important to the reliability of Scripture. However, the addition of the favor of the Holy Spirit and the resurrection from the dead were intended to be unassailable proof, in real-time, as to the veracity of Jesus' claim to be the one and only Son of God.

Dec 13

Will be the Son of God

⁷ **I will tell of the decree: The Lord said to me, "You are my Son; today I have begotten you.**

Psalms 2:7 (ESV)

---------∝---------

A decree is a declaration by a person or group who has authority in the matter. In this verse, God is the one making the declaration or decree. Here we have God giving a glimpse of the future according to His plan. There would be a Son of God and God would recognize and declare Him to the world.

Dec 14

God's Son

[16] And when Jesus was baptized, immediately he went up from the water, and behold, the heavens were opened to him, and he saw the Spirit of God descending like a dove and coming to rest on him; [17] and behold, a voice from heaven said, "This is my beloved Son, with whom I am well pleased."

Matt 3:16-17 (ESV)

———————✕———————

God made the declaration concerning His Son when John baptized Jesus to "fulfill all righteousness." This was a public forum and all who were present heard it. He even used a visual aid in the descending dove! Can you imagine witnessing this? How could any of the people seeing this doubt that Jesus was the long awaited Son of God? Oh,
to have been there...

Dec 15

A Ministry Described

⁴ Say to those who have an anxious heart, "Be strong; fear not! Behold, your God will come with vengeance, with the recompense of God. He will come and save you." ⁵ Then the eyes of the blind shall be opened, and the ears of the deaf unstopped;

Isaiah 35:4-5 (ESV)

In recent years an outlook or worldview came about telling people not to worry about things and not to take things so seriously. That everything will work out and to just sit back and be happy. It almost sounds like, "Be strong; fear not!" doesn't it? However, there is a rather large difference between this worldview and this passage of Scripture. This worldview encourages people to not take things seriously, but does not offer any reasons as to why you should be happy.
The Scripture passage, on the other hand, does expound on the why – "God will come with vengeance" – and tells you what He is going to do – "save you" – and, further, it offers verifiable bonifides – "the eyes of the blind shall be opened, and the ears of the deaf unstopped!" In short, Scripture offers HOPE where this worldview does not.
So, be strong and fear not!

Dec 16

The Ministry Revealed

² Now when John heard in prison about the deeds of the Christ, he sent word by his disciples ³ and said to him, "Are you the one who is to come, or shall we look for another?" ⁴ And Jesus answered them, "Go and tell John what you hear and see: ⁵ the blind receive their sight and the lame walk, lepers are cleansed and the deaf hear, and the dead are raised up, and the poor have good news preached to them.

Matt 11:2-5 (ESV)

―――――◯×―――――

In this fallen world, doubt is easy to come by and Satan stirs it as much as he can. Even John the Baptist, of whom Jesus said "Truly, I say to you, among those born of women there has arisen no one greater than John the Baptist," experienced times of doubt – and he was there when the dove descended and God spoke identifying Jesus as His Son. How much more can our doubts arise, being so far removed from the time of that miracle? But Jesus' assurances to John are our assurances as well. He pointed John, and points us, to the Old Testament prophecy: "the blind receive their sight ... and the deaf hear." Jesus was reminding John, and us, that the Father and Son know what they are doing, it is going according to plan, and we can trust in them. Rest friends, all is well.

The wages of sin is death.

Spiritual death.

Eternal separation from God.

But fear not.

God is sovereign.

Trust in His plan.

His Son will pay our debt.

Dec 17

Prophecy of Sacrificial Atonement (Messiah's Death)

⁵ But he was wounded for our transgressions; he was crushed for our iniquities; upon him was the chastisement that brought us peace, and with his stripes we are healed.

Isaiah 53:5 (ESV)

The Jewish sacrificial system was set up in a way to teach mankind many things. Among them – that there were consequences for sin and that the atonement (satisfaction) for those sins required blood. When mankind sinned, something had to die. But the sacrifices in the Old Testament were not wholly adequate because they had to be repeated each time the sin was committed and because the blood of animals could not cover the sins of mankind. Only the blood of mankind can atone for the sins of mankind and only a perfect sacrifice could satisfy God's perfect justice. So God sent His Son, fully God *AND* fully man — the only perfect sacrifice. God, the Son, would die so that we could be justified and our sins atoned for.

Dec 18

Crucifixion

⁶ For while we were still weak, at the right time Christ died for the ungodly. ⁷ For one will scarcely die for a righteous person—though perhaps for a good person one would dare even to die— ⁸ but God shows his love for us in that while we were still sinners, Christ died for us. ⁹ Since, therefore, we have now been justified by his blood, much more shall we be saved by him from the wrath of God. ¹⁰ For if while we were enemies we were reconciled to God by the death of his Son, much more, now that we are reconciled, shall we be saved by his life. ¹¹ More than that, we also rejoice in God through our Lord Jesus Christ, through whom we have now received reconciliation.

Romans 5:6-11 (ESV)

How far out of your way would you go to help a family member? A friend? A stranger? For many, the answers to the above questions would be positive, but decreasing in the amount of effort put forth or risk taken. What about someone who had hurt you or a member of your family? How far out of your way would you go to help them? This sheds a very different light on the question, doesn't it? Since Adam's sin in the Garden, and through that sin, all humans have been born with a sin nature. We were God's enemies. Yet He went very far out of His way to help us – He sent His Son to save and redeem us even though He knew it would require His death. How does one measure that amount of love? Creation cannot contain it!

———⸻———

The Son of God died.

The Father laid His wrath upon Him.

But fear not.

God is sovereign.

Trust in His plan.

His Son rose to live again and become our Hope.

Dec 19

The Promise of Resurrection

¹⁰ For you will not abandon my soul to Sheol, or let your holy one see corruption.

Psalms 16:10 (ESV)

This promise relates to the curse God laid upon the serpent in the Garden of Eden: the woman's offspring, Jesus, will bruise Satan's head and Satan will bruise Jesus' heel. With Jesus' death on the cross, Satan must have thought he had won, and, if Jesus had remained in the grave, he would have, but Satan didn't even know what the game was nor what events Jesus' death set into motion. God had no plans to abandon Jesus in the grave. Quite the contrary. With Jesus' death, Satan had bruised Jesus' heel and set the stage for Jesus to deal the fatal blow to Satan's head – He would rise from the grave and conquer death!

Dec 20

Christ is Resurrected

⁶ And he said to them, "Do not be alarmed. You seek Jesus of Nazareth, who was crucified. He has risen; he is not here. See the place where they laid him.

Mark 16:6 (ESV)

Imagine you were attending a closed-casket funeral and, when the casket was opened up for everyone to say their last goodbyes, the body was not there? How would that make you feel? Would you be alarmed? Angry? Would you despair? Everyone who dies leaves behind a body, a dead husk, right? Even those who lived in the beginning and had enormously long lives still died – except for Enoch and Elijah. It is the way of things. We are born, we live our lives, we die, we are buried, and our bodies decay. But not Jesus! He is the one we read about in Psalms 16:10 – His body did not see corruption (decay) because He did not stay dead! It was important that His disciples saw that He had risen not only because the Old Testament prophets foretold it, but because Jesus foretold it as well. It is also important from the standpoint of our Christian faith. Without the resurrection, we would have no hope and our faith would be empty and worthless. The crucifixion and the resurrection are inseparable parts of God's plan of salvation for mankind. Yes, Jesus died and was buried, but then He rose from the grave. Hallelujah!

───────⊸⊂───────

How would the Son of the Creator of the universe – the King of kings and Lord of lords – enter creation?

As a conqueror with riches?

No. As a baby in a stable in Bethlehem.

But fear not.

God is sovereign.

Trust in His plan.

Dec 21

Born of a Virgin

[14] Therefore the Lord himself will give you a sign. Behold, the virgin shall conceive and bear a son, and shall call his name Immanuel.

Isaiah 7:14 (ESV)

There are many signs that we can see in our daily lives: some are small while others are big. In nature, storm clouds on the horizon can be the harbinger of rain and a dark "wooly worm" is supposed to indicate a cold winter. Along the interstate, signs inform drivers what the next exit is and how many miles away towns are. A sign is merely a way of communicating something to others.

When God gives a sign to us, it is usually significant and magnificent. A rainbow is the sign given to us from God to assure us that He will never again destroy the earth with rain. The sun, moon, and stars were given to indicate the passing of the seasons. And the universe itself is a sign of the glory and majesty of God. Through His prophet Isaiah, God told the world what the sign would be when He would begin the salvation of creation – and it was spectacular! A "virgin shall conceive!" How wondrous is that?! He would do something that had never been done before. Ever since Adam and Eve, all people had a physical mother and father, but not God's Son! He would be born of a virgin! He was to be the "second Adam" and through Him salvation would come.

Dec 22

The Virgin Mary

²⁶ In the sixth month the angel Gabriel was sent from God to a city of Galilee named Nazareth, ²⁷ to a virgin betrothed to a man whose name was Joseph, of the house of David. And the virgin's name was Mary. ²⁸ And he came to her and said, "Greetings, O favored one, the Lord is with you!" ²⁹ But she was greatly troubled at the saying, and tried to discern what sort of greeting this might be. ³⁰ And the angel said to her, "Do not be afraid, Mary, for you have found favor with God. ³¹ And behold, you will conceive in your womb and bear a son, and you shall call his name Jesus. ³² He will be great and will be called the Son of the Most High. And the Lord God will give to him the throne of his father David, ³³ and he will reign over the house of Jacob forever, and of his kingdom there will be no end." ³⁴ And Mary said to the angel, "How will this be, since I am a virgin?" ³⁵ And the angel answered her, "The Holy Spirit will come upon you, and the power of the Most High will overshadow you; therefore the child to be born will be called holy —
the Son of God.

Luke 1:26-35 (ESV)

Many people who believe in creation have a problem with the virgin birth. This I do not understand. If they can believe that God created the universe, how can they not understand that God can intervene in His own creation. The virgin birth plays a significant role in God's plan of redemption. Human procreation has been the way of things, since the beginning of creation. Adam sinned and brought the curse of the Fall upon all mankind and everyone born since has inherited this curse. But Jesus was different. He did not have an earthly father and therefore did not inherit the blight that is called "original sin." His father was the Holy Spirit making Him both God and man. Truly named Immanuel, which means God with us.

Dec 23

To Be Born In Bethlehem

² But you, O Bethlehem Ephrathah, who are too little to be among the clans of Judah, from you shall come forth for me one who is to be ruler in Israel, whose origin is from of old, from ancient days.

Micah 5:2 (ESV)

———————⚭———————

This is the passage quoted to Herod in Matthew 2:6 by the chief priests and scribes in Jerusalem when the wise men came from the east seeking the one who had "been born king of the Jews." There is no record of debate as to who was being referred to and it should be noted that Herod did not ask what king they were talking about. Instead, he asked the religious leaders "where the Christ was to be born" and they told him, Bethlehem – again with no debate.
They knew who the wise men were seeking and, and from this verse, they also knew that the one who was born was the one promised from the beginning – the one "whose origin is from old, from ancient days."

Dec 24

Joseph and Mary Travel To Bethlehem

¹ In those days a decree went out from Caesar Augustus that all the world should be registered. ² This was the first registration when Quirinius was governor of Syria. ³ And all went to be registered, each to his own town. ⁴ And Joseph also went up from Galilee, from the town of Nazareth, to Judea, to the city of David, which is called Bethlehem, because he was of the house and lineage of David, ⁵ to be registered with Mary, his betrothed, who was with child.

Luke 2:1-5 (ESV)

This is a beautiful example of the sovereignty of God. Have you ever thought about the phrase "it just so happened?" If the phrase "it just so happened" is applied to this passage it would flow something like this: it just so happened that Mary, while she just so happened to be pregnant with Jesus, just so happened to be engaged to Joseph who just so happened to be of the lineage of David when, it just so happened, the first registration of people was called for by Caesar Augustus and, to be properly registered, it just so happened that everyone must return to their home town, which for Joseph just so happened to be Bethlehem, which just so happened to be the town the prophet Micah said the Son of God would be born in. Hmmmm.... Sovereignty anyone?

Hallelujah!

The Lord was coming!

---∝---

Construction on the bridge to Redemption was about to begin!

Dec 25

The Birth of Christ

⁶ And while they were there, the time came for her to give birth. ⁷ And she gave birth to her firstborn son and wrapped him in swaddling cloths and laid him in a manger, because there was no place for them in the inn. ⁸ And in the same region there were shepherds out in the field, keeping watch over their flock by night. ⁹ And an angel of the Lord appeared to them, and the glory of the Lord shone around them, and they were filled with fear. ¹⁰ And the angel said to them, "Fear not, for behold, I bring you good news of a great joy that will be for all the people. ¹¹ For unto you is born this day in the city of David a Savior, who is Christ the Lord. ¹² And this will be a sign for you: you will find a baby wrapped in swaddling cloths and lying in a manger." ¹³ And suddenly there was with the angel a multitude of the heavenly host praising God and saying, ¹⁴ "Glory to God in the highest, and on earth peace among those with whom he is pleased!"

Luke 2:6-14 (ESV)

In the birth of Christ, God planted His standard in the ground. Here the stand would be made. Here He showed Satan the limits of his domain and here He Called all His children to come to Him through His one and only Son. His Son came into creation not as royalty, but as a baby born to the wife of a common laborer. He came not to conquer the world, but to save it. He came not to set up an earthly kingdom, but to pay for our sins and to beat death. He came to open the way to God and to offer salvation to all who will hear Him. He came for you and He came for me. Can you hear Him Calling?

Hallelujah!

The Lord has come!

The bridge to Redemption is completed!

Can you hear Him Calling you?

Do you hear Him Calling you?

If you do, the road to heaven is open to you. This road can be found in Scripture.

It is called The Roman Road.

Dec 26

The Roman Road

[23] for all have sinned and fall short of the glory of God,
Romans 3:23 (ESV)

[8] but God shows his love for us in that while we were still sinners, Christ died for us.
Romans 5:8 (ESV)

[23] For the wages of sin is death, but the free gift of God is eternal life in Christ Jesus our Lord.
Romans 6:23 (ESV)

[30] And those whom he predestined he also called, and those whom he called he also justified, and those whom he justified he also glorified.
Romans 8:30 (ESV)

[9] because, if you confess with your mouth that Jesus is Lord and believe in your heart that God raised him from the dead, you will be saved.
Romans 10:9 (ESV)

Sin entered creation through Adam. This is called the Fall and every person born since has been born with the stain of this Sin on their lives. It is called Original Sin. With this Sin nature, we cannot please God and we fall short of His perfection. There is nothing we can "do" to change this. All are born into His wrath.

But God knew this and planned to send His Son to die on the cross to pay the debt (consequences) of the sin of those He would Call. And in doing so, He showed how much He loved us because He did this while we still had the stain of Original Sin, Adam's sin, on our lives.

God is perfect and cannot allow sin into heaven. The wages (what we earn) of sin can only be paid with death. His Son came to die in our place so that God's perfect justice would be satisfied. Our debt (bill) is paid in full through the Son's perfect sacrifice and the result is eternal life.

God can change our hearts and Call us to salvation. This is Grace – the "free gift." If this happens, we will believe in our hearts and in our souls that Jesus is Lord and we will confess this with our mouths freely to all people!

So, now what?!

If you followed The Roman Road presented on December 26—if you asked Jesus for salvation and to be Lord of your life, what happens now?

God knows you and wants you to know Him.

He tells you how in the special revelation of His Word...

Dec 27

Read and Study Scripture

[16] **All Scripture is breathed out by God and profitable for teaching, for reproof, for correction, and for training in righteousness,**
2 Tim 3:16 (ESV)

[105] **Your word is a lamp to my feet and a light to my path.**
Psalms 119:105 (ESV)

[4] **But he answered, "It is written, " 'Man shall not live by bread alone, but by every word that comes from the mouth of God.' "**
Matt 4:4 (ESV)

[11] **I have stored up your word in my heart, that I might not sin against you.**
Psalms 119:11 (ESV)

Truth, no matter how much it is hated, maligned, challenged, or ignored, does not change. You can accept it, ignore it, or try to redefine it, but you cannot change it. Too often people confuse perception and opinion with truth. God's Word is absolute truth and as such can be relied on for learning, teaching, training, and correcting.

The Word of God is the instruction book for life. It tells us how to live and how to die. In it God tells us who He is and who we are. And most importantly, it shows us the path to take to keep us from spending eternity in hell.

While the Hebrews wandered in the wilderness, God gave them manna from heaven to eat. This allowed them to focus on God while He taught them that they could trust Him with their very existence.

Satan is a master at distractions. He wants nothing more than for you to focus on the things you should be trusting God to provide. David understood this and shows us how to combat these distractions—read and study God's Word and "hide it in your heart" so that you can call upon it when needed just as Jesus did when He was tempted by Satan.

In His Word, God tells us about Himself.

Who He is and what He expects of His people.

He also wants us to get to know Him on a personal level.

---ᗅ---

Scripture says that we can speak to God through prayer and that He will hear our prayers. Asked by the disciples, Jesus tells us how to pray.

He wants to hear from you...

Dec 28

Pray Then Like This ...

⁹ Pray then like this:
"Our Father in heaven, hallowed be your name. ¹⁰ Your kingdom come, your will be done, on earth as it is in heaven. ¹¹ Give us this day our daily bread, ¹² and forgive us our debts, as we also have forgiven our debtors. ¹³ And lead us not into temptation, but deliver us from evil."

Matt 6:9-13 (ESV)

In the Psalms, you will find many beautiful examples of prayers to God, but in Matthew 6:9-13, Jesus supplies us with what is commonly called the Lord's Prayer. It is not intended to be repeated verbatim, but rather it is a step-by-step recipe or model. It can be broken down into 5 sections that we should emphasize in our prayer life:

Verse 9 – acknowledge God's deity and holiness.

Verse 10 – acknowledge God's sovereignty and your submission to it.

Verse 11 – voice your petitions/requests and ask Him to strengthen and sustain you.

Verse 12 – ask for His forgiveness and mercy as you have shown mercy to others.

Verse 13 – ask Him for direction and guidance.

When you pray using this model, pull from and supply details from your bible reading, your pastor's sermons, your everyday life experiences, and current situation.

———⚯———

God knows that we will have problems in life that arise specifically from our being Christians. He warns us of this in:

Luke 6:22-23 and John 15:18-19

The world will hate us because of Jesus Christ, just as they hated the prophets of the Old Testament and as they hated Jesus Himself.

But God has a plan ...

Dec 29

Worship with a Local Body of Believers

[23] Let us hold fast the confession of our hope without wavering, for he who promised is faithful. [24] And let us consider how to stir up one another to love and good works, [25] not neglecting to meet together, as is the habit of some, but encouraging one another, and all the more as you see the Day drawing near.

Heb 10:23-25 (ESV)

God knew it would be difficult to remain faithful in the face of the unrelenting pressure from the non-Christians in the world. So He exhorts (encourages) us to be strong in what we believe and to not waver in our resolve.

He also knew that groups of Christians would be better able to handle this pressure so He tells us to meet together with others Christians. When we do this, we:

- Will have the support of others when we go through trials,

- Will have the blessing of helping others through their trials,

- Will have the opportunity to bless others with good works and deeds.

Additionally, He knew that the cultural (societal) pressure would continue to get worse as the second coming of Jesus Christ grew nearer and stressed the need of meeting together even more in the last days.

So what now?

You have received Christ as your Savior, you are reading and studying Scripture, praying, and attending church.

Is this all there is?

Not hardly!

God did not die on the cross for you alone nor for you to remain silent!

He has a blessing in store for you, but it may be outside your comfort zone.

Dec 30

Tell Others of the Gift You Have Been Given

[13] "You are the salt of the earth, but if salt has lost its taste, how shall its saltiness be restored? It is no longer good for anything except to be thrown out and trampled under people's feet. [14] "You are the light of the world. A city set on a hill cannot be hidden. [15] Nor do people light a lamp and put it under a basket, but on a stand, and it gives light to all in the house. [16] In the same way, let your light shine before others, so that they may see your good works and give glory to your Father who is in heaven.

Matt 5:13-16 (ESV)

If you have indeed received Salvation from our Lord, you will have a burning desire to tell others to turn from the path of sin and wrath. That God, in Christ, Calls them to salvation. This is a wondrous thing!

God has chosen to allow us the blessing of being a part of the salvation of others. Not that we are responsible for their actual salvation, but we are to show them the way by sharing the gospel we have been given. We do this by witnessing (telling others of our salvation experience) and by living our lives in such a way that they will see we are different.

You may have heard it said that we are to be "the salt of the earth." This means that, just as salt was once used to preserve meat, God intends for Christians to be a part of the "preservation" of those in His creation.

We have been saved from an eternity in Hell by the Light of the world (Jesus Christ) and we must not hide that Light from others. We are to be beacons to show the path of salvation to those who are lost!

Is it enough to tell others of your salvation?

God doesn't think so.

He not only wants us to share – He wants us to serve!

In Matthew 25:34-40, Jesus tells us -

---⋈---

We are to feed the hungry, give drink to the thirsty, welcome the stranger, clothe the naked, visit the sick and those in prison.

And He <u>shows</u> us this through His service...

Dec 31

Serving Others

[3] Jesus, knowing that the Father had given all things into his hands, and that he had come from God and was going back to God, [4] rose from supper. He laid aside his outer garments, and taking a towel, tied it around his waist. [5] Then he poured water into a basin and began to wash the disciples' feet and to wipe them with the towel that was wrapped around him.

John 13:3-5 (ESV)

Jesus, the Christ, the Son of God, God incarnate washed the feet of His disciples.

In the days of Jesus, the choice of footwear was limited, essentially sandals and slippers. When walking outside on dusty or muddy roads, people's feet got understandably dirty and it was the job of the servant of the house they entered to wash the feet of travelers.

As you might guess, this was not the most desirable position in the household. So, when Jesus washed His disciples feet, He was performing one of the lowliest jobs of a servant and sending a message to His disciples and to us – this is what we should do: serve others!

Who are we to say that "others should serve while I am being served?"

Jesus, the Christ, the Son of God, God incarnate washed the feet of His disciples.

What are some ways you could serve others at your church or in your community in the coming week... month... year?

There is one more thing God wants you to do.

He wants you to learn math.

Not the "new" math you hear about, but rather "God's" math.

"Be fruitful and multiply."

For Adam and Eve, this was a physical mandate. For us, it is spiritual.

They were to make babies, we are to make disciples.

Jan 1

The Great Commission

[18] And Jesus came and said to them, "All authority in heaven and on earth has been given to me. [19] Go therefore and make disciples of all nations, baptizing them in the name of the Father and of the Son and of the Holy Spirit, [20] teaching them to observe all that I have commanded you. And behold, I am with you always, to the end of the age."

Matt 28:18-20 (ESV)

A commission (a charge or a job) was about to be given, but commissions require authority and Jesus wanted them, and us, to know what authority He had to give this commission and what the limits of that authority were. So He started with this: "All authority in heaven and on earth has been given to me."

What authority did He have? All of it!

What were the limits? Absolutely none!

Who did this authority come from? God, because only He had all of the authority to give.

We have been commissioned to:
- Make disciples
- Baptize them
- Teach them

Some will say that "Go" was left off of this list, but it was not. "Go" is rendered by some scholars to be "as you are going" or "as you go about your daily lives."

So we are to do these things as part of our everyday lives and Jesus will be with us – always!

So, you have your commission.

The King of kings has charged you with the expansion of His kingdom.

Who are you to be given this task?

Have you done great things?

---⋈---

Is that why you have been chosen?

No.

You are a sinner, just like me, saved by the Grace of God. Bought by the blood of His Son.

Trust in Him and He will see you through.

Notes

Notes

www.ingramcontent.com/pod-product-compliance
Ingram Content Group UK Ltd.
Pitfield, Milton Keynes, MK11 3LW, UK
UKHW041949230426
12048UKWH00008B/238